# Guide to Spring

## Practical Guide

A. De Quattro

Copyright © 2024

Practical Guide

# 1. Introduction to Spring

Spring is one of the most popular and widely used frameworks in the Java ecosystem for enterprise application development. Designed to simplify the development and implementation of applications, Spring offers a suite of tools and technologies to handle the complexities associated with modern application development, such as transaction management, data access, security, and more. In this document, we will explore in detail what Spring is, its architecture, and the advantages it offers to developers and businesses.

#### 1.1 What is Spring?

**Definition and History**

Spring is an open-source framework for the Java platform, initially created by Rod Johnson in 2003. The primary goal of Spring from its inception was to address the complexity of Java Enterprise Edition (JEE, previously J2EE) applications by providing a simpler and more flexible object-oriented programming (OOP) model. Spring is designed to be modular, meaning developers can use only the components they need, reducing the overhead and complexity of the project.

Since its early versions, Spring has introduced various software development paradigms that have become standards in the Java world. One such paradigm is Inversion of Control (IoC), which promotes the use of external dependencies managed by a container, allowing developers to avoid tight coupling between classes.

#### 1.2 Spring and the Inversion of Control (IoC) Pattern

The concept of IoC is central to Spring and refers to the practice of delegating the control of the execution flow of an application to a container. In the context of Spring, this container is called the Spring IoC Container. In practice, the framework handles the creation and injection of dependencies between various components of the application.

Spring implements IoC primarily through the use of the Dependency Injection (DI) pattern, which can be of two main types:

- **Constructor Injection:** Dependencies are passed via the class constructor.

- **Setter Injection:** Dependencies are injected through setter methods.

This mechanism allows for better maintainability and testability of applications, as dependencies can be easily modified or replaced during testing.

#### 1.3 Spring and the Aspect-Oriented

Programming (AOP) Pattern

Another key concept in Spring is Aspect-Oriented Programming (AOP). AOP is a methodology that allows for the separation of cross-cutting concerns (such as logging, transaction management, and security) from the core application logic. With AOP, developers can define aspects that are executed around specific methods without having to modify the main source code. This approach improves modularity and reduces code duplication.

#### 1.4 Main Components of Spring

Spring consists of several modules, each dedicated to a specific aspect of application development. The main modules include:

- **Spring Core:** Contains the fundamental features of IoC and DI.
- **Spring AOP:** Supports aspect-oriented

programming.

- **Spring Data:** Provides simplified integration with databases, allowing data access and transaction management.

- **Spring MVC:** A module for creating web applications based on the Model-View-Controller pattern.

- **Spring Security:** Offers advanced security features for authentication and authorization.

- **Spring Boot:** A variant of Spring that allows the creation of standalone Spring applications with a "convention over configuration" approach.

### 2. Spring Architecture

The architecture of Spring is based on a series of modular layers that can be used independently or combined to create complex applications. Generally, Spring's architecture can be divided into four main levels:

#### 2.1 Core Level

The Core Container is the heart of the Spring architecture and provides the fundamental functionalities of bean management, IoC, and DI. The main modules in this layer include:

- **Spring Core:** The core of the framework, responsible for configuration and management of beans in the IoC container.

- **Spring Beans:** Provides all the classes and interfaces necessary for bean management, XML configuration, and DI implementation.

- **Spring Context:** Extends the Beans module, providing a context-oriented framework that enables advanced bean lifecycle management and integration with other technologies.

- **Spring Expression Language (SpEL):** An expressive language for dynamic manipulation of beans and their properties, commonly used for XML configuration and Java annotation.

The IoC container manages the creation, configuration, and lifecycle of objects or "beans" within the application. Spring provides both an XML-based approach to bean configuration and an annotation-based approach, making development faster and more intuitive.

#### 2.2 Web Level

The Spring Web module is designed to support web application development, particularly based on servlets and HTTP requests. The main components of this layer include:

- **Spring MVC:** The Model-View-Controller framework of Spring, which facilitates the development of web applications according to the MVC paradigm. It manages HTTP requests and separates business logic (model) from the presentation (view) and control (controller).

- **Spring WebFlux:** A reactive framework

introduced in recent versions of Spring, designed to build non-blocking and asynchronous applications. WebFlux is based on the reactive programming model, offering support for frameworks like Project Reactor and RxJava.

Spring MVC and WebFlux are the two main options for building web applications in Spring. While Spring MVC is traditionally synchronous, WebFlux introduces a non-blocking approach, particularly useful for applications that need to handle a large number of simultaneous connections, such as streaming applications or microservices.

#### 2.3 Data Access Level

Spring provides a wide range of tools for managing data access and integration with relational and non-relational databases. This level includes the following main modules:

- **Spring JDBC:** Simplifies interaction with relational databases through JDBC, efficiently managing database connections, SQL queries, and result mapping.

- **Spring ORM:** Provides integration with object-relational mapping (ORM) technologies such as Hibernate, JPA, and MyBatis, facilitating the persistence of Java objects in databases.

- **Spring Data:** A project aimed at simplifying data access in Java, providing abstractions for relational and non-relational databases, including MongoDB, Cassandra, Redis, and more. Spring Data also includes native integration with JPA, making it extremely easy to work with entities and repositories.

The data access level of Spring offers tremendous flexibility, allowing developers to choose the persistence technology best suited to their needs. Additionally, thanks to Spring Data, repository implementation becomes automated and highly configurable through annotations.

#### 2.4 AOP and Security Level

The Aspect-Oriented Programming (AOP) level provides functionalities that allow for the separation of cross-cutting concerns from the core application code. Spring AOP enables the implementation of aspects such as:

- **Transaction Management:** Spring allows for the definition of declarative transactions that are managed automatically by the framework, eliminating the need for manual transaction handling in application code.

- **Security:** Through Spring Security, it is possible to easily implement authentication and authorization mechanisms, protecting applications from unauthorized access.

- **Logging:** With the help of AOP, it is possible to implement logging and monitoring mechanisms transparently within the application.

### 3. Advantages of Using Spring

Adopting Spring as a development framework brings numerous benefits, ranging from code simplification to advanced transaction and application infrastructure management. Some of the key advantages include:

#### 3.1 Modularity and Flexibility

One of Spring's main strengths is its modular architecture. Developers can choose and use only the modules they need, avoiding unnecessary component overhead. This flexibility allows Spring to be used in a wide range of scenarios, from simple data access to complex microservices systems. Furthermore, Spring easily integrates with other technologies, enabling developers to build applications with the most suitable combination of tools and libraries for the specific case.

#### 3.2 Inversion of Control and Dependency Injection

The adoption of the IoC pattern and DI significantly reduces the amount of tight coupling between application components. This results in more modular, maintainable, and testable code. The separation of responsibilities between components allows for greater flexibility and facilitates the writing of unit and integration tests, as dependencies can be easily replaced with mocks during testing.

#### 3.3 Support for Transactions

Spring greatly simplifies transaction management by allowing for declarative transactions that are automatically managed by the framework. This means developers do not need to handle transactions manually in the application code, reducing boilerplate and potential for errors.

#### 3.4 Integration with Various Technologies

Spring provides excellent integration with a variety of technologies, including databases, messaging systems, and external APIs. Its modularity ensures that developers can incorporate only the necessary components for their specific needs, making it easier to build robust and scalable applications.

## 2.Setting Up the Development Environment

Setting up a development environment to work with a framework like **Spring** is a critical step to ensure an efficient and productive workflow. In this document, we will explore the necessary system requirements, the steps for installing **Java** and **Maven**, and how to configure a **Spring** project from scratch.

### System Requirements

Before proceeding with the installation and configuration of Java, Maven, and Spring, it is important to ensure that the system meets the basic requirements. Although Spring can run on a wide range of hardware and software configurations, an ideal development environment requires specific resources and pre-installed software.

#### 1.1. Hardware Requirements

- **CPU**: A multi-core processor (Intel i5 or higher or an equivalent AMD) is recommended to handle multiple processes simultaneously, such as the Java compiler, the web server, the IDE, and Maven.

- **RAM**: 8 GB of RAM is the minimum recommended for a smooth development environment, but to handle multiple Spring projects, at least 16 GB of RAM is advisable.

- **Disk Space**: The Spring framework, along with the various necessary tools and libraries, requires a decent amount of disk space. A minimum of 10 GB is recommended for active development, but having more available space (at least 50 GB) is advisable for future updates and projects.

- **Internet Connection**: A stable internet connection is necessary to download Maven, dependencies, plugins, and libraries required for Spring.

#### 1.2. Software Requirements

- **Operating System**: Spring is compatible with all major operating systems, including:

  - Windows 10/11

  - macOS 10.14 (Mojave) or later

  - Linux distributions like Ubuntu 20.04 LTS, CentOS 8, or Fedora 34.


- **Java Development Kit (JDK)**: Spring requires an installed JDK. For most modern projects, it is recommended to use **JDK 11** or later (for example, JDK 17, which is an LTS version).


- **Apache Maven**: A build system like **Maven** is essential for managing project dependencies and simplifying the build process.


- **IDE**: While it's possible to work with Spring using just a text editor and command-line tools, an **Integrated Development Environment (IDE)** greatly simplifies the development process. The most popular IDEs for Spring development include:

  - **IntelliJ IDEA** (Ultimate edition, which provides full Spring support)

  - **Eclipse IDE** with the Spring Tool Suite (STS) plugin

  - **Visual Studio Code** with Java and Spring extensions.

#### 1.3. Dependencies and Additional Components

- **Git**: Spring is often used by development teams collaborating remotely, so having Git installed is essential for version control.

- **Docker** (optional): Docker is increasingly used to containerize Spring applications, especially in microservices-based workflows. If you plan to containerize your applications or run local databases in containers, it's helpful to install Docker.

### Installing Java and Maven

#### 2.1. Installing the Java Development Kit (JDK)

The first step to setting up a Spring development environment is installing the **Java Development Kit (JDK)**. Below are detailed steps for installing the JDK on various operating systems.

##### 2.1.1. Installing on Windows

1. **Download the JDK**: Visit the official Oracle or OpenJDK website (https://jdk.java.net/) to download the latest version of Java (e.g., JDK 17 LTS).

2. **Run the installation file**: After downloading the executable file (.exe), open it to start the installation. Follow the on-screen instructions to complete the process.

3. **Configure the environment variable**:

 - After installation, configure the `JAVA_HOME` environment variable. Go to *Control Panel* > *System* > *Advanced system settings* > *Environment variables*.

 - Create a new system variable called `JAVA_HOME` and set the path to the JDK installation directory (e.g., `C:\Program Files\Java\jdk-17`).

 - Add `%JAVA_HOME%\bin` to the `PATH` system variable.


4. **Verify the installation**: Open the command prompt and type:

```bash
java -version
```

This command should return the installed Java version.

##### 2.1.2. Installing on macOS

1. **Download the JDK**: You can download the JDK directly from the Oracle website or via Homebrew, a package manager for macOS.

   To install via Homebrew, run:

   ```bash
   brew install openjdk@17
   ```

2. **Configure the environment variable**:

   - Open the terminal and add the JDK path to the `.zshrc` file (or `.bash_profile` if using bash).

   ```bash
   export JAVA_HOME=$(/usr/libexec/java_home)
   export PATH=$JAVA_HOME/bin:$PATH
   ```

```

3. **Verify the installation**: Type in the terminal:

   ```bash
   java -version
   ```

   This command should return the installed Java version.

##### 2.1.3. Installing on Linux

1. **Install via apt** (on Ubuntu):

   ```bash
   sudo apt update
   sudo apt install openjdk-17-jdk
   ```

2. **Configure the environment variable**:
   ```

Add the following line to the `.bashrc` or `.zshrc` file:

```bash
export JAVA_HOME=/usr/lib/jvm/java-17-openjdk-amd64
export PATH=$JAVA_HOME/bin:$PATH
```

3. **Verify the installation**:

```bash
java -version
```

#### 2.2. Installing Apache Maven

Apache Maven is a build and dependency management tool that simplifies managing libraries and plugins needed for Spring application development. The Maven installation varies slightly depending on the operating system.

##### 2.2.1. Installing on Windows

1. **Download Maven**: Visit the official Apache Maven website (https://maven.apache.org/download.cgi) and download the binary version of Maven in zip format.

2. **Extract the file**: Extract the contents of the zip file to a directory of your choice (e.g., `C:\Program Files\Maven`).

3. **Configure the environment variable**:

   - Go to *Control Panel* > *System* > *Advanced system settings* > *Environment variables*.

   - Create a new system variable called `MAVEN_HOME` and set the path to the Maven directory (e.g., `C:\Program Files\Maven`).

- Add `%MAVEN_HOME%\bin` to the `PATH` system variable.

4. **Verify the installation**: Open the command prompt and type:

```bash
mvn -version
```

This command should return the installed Maven version.

##### 2.2.2. Installing on macOS

1. **Install via Homebrew**:

```bash
brew install maven
```

2. **Verify the installation**:

```bash
mvn -version
```

##### 2.2.3. Installing on Linux

1. **Install via apt** (on Ubuntu):
   ```bash
   sudo apt update
   sudo apt install maven
   ```

2. **Verify the installation**:
   ```bash
   mvn -version
   ```

### Configuring a Spring Project

Once Java and Maven are installed, you can proceed with setting up your first Spring project. Using **Spring Boot**, a simplified variant of Spring, makes setting up and starting new projects extremely quick. Spring Boot automatically handles complex configurations and provides a range of tools to quickly start a web or enterprise application.

#### 3.1. Using Spring Initializr

The most common method to create a new Spring project is to use **Spring Initializr**, a web interface that allows you to generate a customized project structure.

1. **Access Spring Initializr**: Visit the website [https://start.spring.io/](https://start.spring.io/).

2. **Configure the project**:

- **Project**: Choose `Maven Project` as the build system.

  - **Language**: Select `Java`.

  - **Spring Boot Version**: Select the latest stable version of Spring Boot (e.g., `2.5.4` or `2.6.x`).

  - **Project Metadata**:

    - **Group**: Defines the primary package name of the application (e.g., `com.example`).

    - **Artifact**: The project name (e.g., `demo`).

    - **Name**: Project name (e.g., `Demo`).

    - **Package Name**: The package name will be automatically generated based on the `Group` and `Artifact`.


3. **Add Dependencies**: Add the necessary dependencies for your project. Common dependencies include:

   - **Spring Web**: For developing web applications using Spring MVC.

- **Spring Data JPA**: For integrating with relational databases using the Java Persistence API.

- **H2 Database**: An in-memory database for development and testing purposes.

4. **Generate the project**: Once the details are configured, click "Generate." This will download a ZIP file containing the project structure.

5. **Import into IDE**: Extract the ZIP file and import the project into your IDE (IntelliJ, Eclipse, or Visual Studio Code). If using IntelliJ:

  - Go to *File* > *New* > *Project from Existing Sources*.

  - Select the extracted directory and follow the instructions to import the Maven project.

####

## 3.2. Running the Spring Application

Once the project is imported into your IDE, you can run the application by executing the `main` method in the `DemoApplication` class.

```java
public class DemoApplication {
    public static void main(String[] args) {
        SpringApplication.run(DemoApplication.class, args);
    }
}
```

Alternatively, you can run the application using the Maven command in your terminal:

```bash
mvn spring-boot:run
```

If everything is configured correctly, you should see a message that Spring Boot has started successfully, and your application will be running on `http://localhost:8080`.

Setting up a Spring development environment requires installing essential tools like Java, Maven, and an IDE. Following the steps outlined in this document will help you establish a robust setup, enabling you to start developing applications with the Spring framework effectively.

# 3. Fundamental Concepts of Spring

The **Spring** framework is one of the most popular in the Java world due to its ability to simplify the development of complex applications. Key principles that make Spring such a powerful and efficient framework include **Inversion of Control (IoC)**, **Dependency Injection (DI)**, and the **application context**. These concepts are the foundation of how Spring operates and are essential for understanding how it manages the lifecycle and integration of components.

In this section, we will examine in detail the concepts of Inversion of Control, Dependency Injection, and the Spring application context, exploring how they work together to facilitate development and make applications more modular, testable, and flexible.

### Inversion of Control (IoC)

#### 1.1. Definition of Inversion of Control

**Inversion of Control (IoC)** is a software design principle where the flow of an application is no longer controlled by the developer but delegated to a framework or container. In other words, instead of manually creating object instances and managing their dependencies, the developer entrusts this task to a framework like Spring.

The IoC concept is broad and can be implemented in various ways, but in Spring, it is mainly achieved through **Dependency Injection (DI)**. IoC allows for the separation of responsibilities between components, facilitating the management of dependencies among complex objects and improving code testability.

A simple way to explain IoC is by considering the shift in responsibility for object management. In a traditional application, the programmer's code directly instantiates the objects it needs. In an IoC-based system, the task of creating and managing objects is handled by the IoC container (such as the **Spring IoC Container**), which injects the required dependencies at the appropriate time.

#### 1.2. Advantages of Inversion of Control

Adopting IoC offers several significant advantages, including:

- **Increased modularity**: By separating responsibilities, the code becomes more modular, and individual components can be easily isolated.

- **Improved maintainability**: Since dependency control is delegated to Spring, the code is less coupled, making it easier to update or replace individual components without affecting the rest of the system.

- **Better testability**: IoC facilitates the use of techniques such as unit testing, as dependencies can be replaced by **mocks** or **stubs** during tests, without the need to instantiate real objects.

- **Flexibility**: Developers can define application behavior and configuration through external settings, allowing for greater flexibility in adapting the application to different scenarios.

#### 1.3. Types of Inversion of Control

IoC can be implemented in various ways. In Spring, the most common form of IoC is Dependency Injection (DI), which we will explore in detail in the next section. However, it's important to note that IoC can also be realized through other methods, such as:

- **Service Locator**: A pattern where an object actively looks up its services from a centralized registry.

- **Event-Driven IoC**: Objects act in response to events rather than direct commands.

Spring primarily implements IoC using Dependency Injection, meaning the framework manages the creation and injection of objects that a component needs to function correctly.

### Dependency Injection (DI)

#### 2.1. What is Dependency Injection?

**Dependency Injection (DI)** is a pattern that implements the IoC principle. DI allows the externalization of the process of creating dependencies between system components. This means that, instead of manually creating or looking up the necessary object instances, the framework (in this case, Spring) automatically injects the required dependencies into a component.

In the context of Spring, a "dependency" is simply another object that a class needs to perform its functions. By injecting dependencies instead of creating them directly, a class can focus on its specific logic, delegating to the framework the management of object creation and lifecycle.

#### 2.2. Types of Dependency Injection

There are various ways to inject dependencies into a component. Spring primarily supports three types of Dependency Injection:

##### 2.2.1. Constructor Injection

Constructor injection is one of the most common methods of DI. Dependencies are provided when the object is created via the constructor. This method is considered the safest, as it ensures that the object is only created when all its dependencies are available.

Example of constructor injection in Spring:

```java
@Component
public class UserService {

    private final UserRepository userRepository;

    // Constructor Injection
    @Autowired
    public UserService(UserRepository userRepository) {
        this.userRepository = userRepository;
    }

    public void performService() {
        userRepository.save(new User());
    }
}
```

```

In this example, `UserRepository` is injected as a dependency into the `UserService` constructor.

##### 2.2.2. Setter Injection

Another way to inject dependencies is through **setter methods**. In this case, Spring injects the dependencies by calling the setter methods on the object after its creation.

Example of setter injection:

```java
@Component
public class UserService {

    private UserRepository userRepository;

```
// Setter Injection
@Autowired
public void setUserRepository(UserRepository userRepository) {
    this.userRepository = userRepository;
}


public void performService() {
    userRepository.save(new User());
}
}
```

This approach is useful when a dependency is optional or can be changed after the object's creation.

##### 2.2.3. Field Injection

Spring also allows direct injection into fields using the `@Autowired` annotation. In this case, Spring injects the dependency directly into the field, bypassing the constructor or setter methods.

Example of field injection:

```java
@Component
public class UserService {

    @Autowired
    private UserRepository userRepository;

    public void performService() {
        userRepository.save(new User());
```

```
    }
}
```

This method is considered less flexible compared to others, as it makes it more challenging to test the object with `mock` or `stub` dependencies without using advanced techniques like **reflection**.

#### 2.3. Lifecycle of Dependencies in Spring

When Spring manages Dependency Injection, it follows a well-defined lifecycle for creating and destroying objects. The **Spring IoC Container** manages this lifecycle, which includes the following stages:

1. **Bean Creation**: When the Spring application starts, the IoC container loads the bean definitions (which can be configured via annotations or XML files) and creates the

object instances.

2. **Dependency Injection**: After the instance is created, the container injects the necessary dependencies into each bean, following the specified configuration.

3. **Bean Initialization**: Once dependencies are injected, beans can perform further initialization tasks, as defined by the `@PostConstruct` annotation or by implementing the `InitializingBean` interface.

4. **Bean Usage**: After the beans are ready, they are used within the application, performing the core tasks of the business logic.

5. **Bean Destruction**: When the application shuts down, the IoC container destroys the beans, invoking any cleanup methods defined by the `@PreDestroy` annotation or the `DisposableBean` interface.

### Spring Application Context

#### 3.1. What is the Application Context?

The **Application Context** is the core of Spring's IoC architecture. It is an interface representing the IoC container that manages the lifecycle of beans, dependencies, and application resources. The application context is responsible for creating and managing all the components of a Spring application, including beans, services, and configurations.

In Spring, the application context not only manages beans but also offers additional features like:

- **Resource management**: The context can access external resources like configuration files, databases, and other sources.

- **Internationalization**: Support for managing messages and resources in multiple languages.

- **Event and listener management**: Allows creating and handling events between components.

- **Application lifecycle integration**: Provides methods to initialize and destroy beans at application startup or shutdown.

#### 3.2. Types of ApplicationContext

Spring provides several types of **ApplicationContext**, each designed to meet specific configuration and environment needs:

- **AnnotationConfigApplicationContext**: Used when configuring a Spring application using only Java annotations, without XML files.

- **ClassPathXmlApplicationContext**: Used to load an application context from an XML file located in the classpath.

- **FileSystemXmlApplicationContext**: Similar to `ClassPathXmlApplicationContext` but allows loading XML configuration files from any file system path.

- **WebApplicationContext**: An extension of `ApplicationContext` for web applications, integrated into web containers like Tomcat or

Jetty.

#### 3.3. Creating an Application Context

In Spring, the application context is created at application startup. If using Spring Boot, this process is managed automatically, but it can still be manually configured in non-Spring Boot applications.

Example of creating an annotation-based application context:

```java
ApplicationContext context = new AnnotationConfigApplicationContext(AppConfig.class);

MyService myService = context.getBean(MyService.class);

myService.performAction();
```

In this example, the context is created using a configuration class annotated (`AppConfig`), and a bean (`MyService`) is retrieved from the context.

#### 3.4. Differences between BeanFactory and ApplicationContext

Spring provides two main interfaces for managing beans: `BeanFactory` and `ApplicationContext`. While both manage beans and their dependencies, there are some fundamental differences between them:

- **BeanFactory**: A basic interface for Spring's IoC container. It is lightweight and suitable for resource-limited scenarios, but it doesn't offer advanced features like event management or internationalization.

- **ApplicationContext**: Extends `BeanFactory` and adds advanced features such as internationalization support, event management, and integration with the application lifecycle.

In most cases, `ApplicationContext` is preferred over `BeanFactory` because it provides a more comprehensive set of features required for

enterprise applications.

---

These three concepts—**Inversion of Control (IoC)**, **Dependency Injection (DI)**, and the **ApplicationContext**—form the foundation of the Spring framework. By understanding how these concepts work, you gain insight into how Spring manages application components, dependencies, and their lifecycles. This knowledge is crucial when building scalable and maintainable applications in the Spring ecosystem.

## 4.Bean Management in Spring

One of the central concepts in the Spring framework is **Bean Management**, which represents the core components of an application. Bean management involves creating, initializing, configuring, and destroying objects, all orchestrated by Spring's **Inversion of Control (IoC) container**. The container handles the automatic injection of necessary dependencies between various application components, ensuring they are used as efficiently as possible.

In this section, we will explore the following aspects of bean management in Spring:

- Defining a bean in Spring
- Bean scopes
- Bean lifecycle

### Defining a Bean in Spring

#### 1.1. What is a Bean?

A **bean** in Spring is an object managed by the IoC container. In other words, a bean is a component of your application that is created, configured, and managed by the IoC container. These objects are "registered" in the container and are ready to be used within the application flow according to their dependencies.

Each bean has a unique identifier (or name) within the container, and its dependencies can be specified through **Dependency Injection (DI)**. Beans are configured using annotations or XML configuration files, depending on the project type or the developer's preferences.

#### 1.2. Declaring a Bean

Beans can be declared in Spring using three

main methods:

- **Annotations**: Using the `@Component` annotation or others like `@Service`, `@Repository`, `@Controller`.

- **Java Configuration**: Using a configuration class annotated with `@Configuration` and defining methods with `@Bean`.

- **XML Configuration**: Defining beans within an XML configuration file.

##### 1.2.1. Declaring via Annotations

The most modern and common way to define a bean in Spring is through the `@Component` annotation. This annotation indicates that the annotated class represents a bean managed by Spring. You can also use specialized annotations like `@Service` for business logic components, `@Repository` for data access components, and `@Controller` for controllers in an MVC-based web application.

Example of using `@Component`:

```java
import org.springframework.stereotype.Component;

@Component
public class MyBean {
    public void doSomething() {
        System.out.println("Hello from MyBean!");
    }
}
```

In this example, the `MyBean` class is declared as a Spring bean. The container will handle the creation and management of this object, making it available for injection into other parts of the application.

##### 1.2.2. Declaring via Java Configuration

Another common method is using a configuration class annotated with `@Configuration`, where beans are defined through methods annotated with `@Bean`. This approach is useful when more detailed configuration is needed or when annotations at the class level cannot be used.

Example of a declaration using `@Configuration`:

```java
import org.springframework.context.annotation.Bean;
import org.springframework.context.annotation.Confi
```

guration;

```java
@Configuration
public class AppConfig {

    @Bean
    public MyBean myBean() {
        return new MyBean();
    }
}
```

Here, the `myBean()` method returns an instance of `MyBean`, which is registered in the Spring context as a bean. The Java configuration approach is very flexible and allows you to define in detail how beans should be created.

##### 1.2.3. Declaring via XML

Configuration

Although XML usage is less common in modern projects, it is still an option. Beans can be defined in an XML configuration file using the `<bean>` tag.

Example of an XML declaration:

```xml
<beans xmlns="http://www.springframework.org/schema/beans"

xmlns:xsi="http://www.w3.org/2001/XMLSchema-instance"

xsi:schemaLocation="http://www.springframework.org/schema/beans

http://www.springframework.org/schema/beans/spring-beans.xsd">
```

```
    <bean id="myBean" class="com.example.MyBean"/>

</beans>
```

In this example, a bean with the identifier `myBean` and the associated class `com.example.MyBean` is defined. This bean will be created and managed by the Spring IoC container.

---

### Bean Scopes

A bean's **scope** in Spring defines the lifecycle and visibility context of the bean within the application. Each bean can have a different scope, determining how and when the bean instance is created, used, and destroyed. Spring offers various types of scopes that can be assigned to beans depending on the application's needs.

#### 2.1. Types of Bean Scopes

The main bean scopes in Spring are:

- **Singleton** (default)
- **Prototype**
- **Request**
- **Session**
- **Application**
- **WebSocket**

##### 2.1.1. Singleton Scope

The **Singleton** scope is the default scope

in Spring. When a bean is configured as a singleton, a single instance of the bean is created for the entire Spring context. Every time that bean is requested, the container returns the same instance.

Example of a singleton scope:

```java
@Component
@Scope("singleton")
public class SingletonBean {
    public void doSomething() {
        System.out.println("Singleton instance");
    }
}
```

In this example, `SingletonBean` will have only one instance for the entire application.

This is useful for components that are stateless or need to be shared across different parts of the application.

Advantages of singleton scope:

- Less memory usage, as only one instance of the bean is created.

- Suitable for stateless or shared components.

Disadvantages:

- Not suitable for stateful components, as all requests use the same instance.

##### 2.1.2. Prototype Scope

The **Prototype** scope creates a new instance of the bean every time it is requested from the IoC container. This means that a new instance is created every time the bean is injected or retrieved.

Example of a prototype scope:

```java
@Component
@Scope("prototype")
public class PrototypeBean {
    public void doSomething() {
        System.out.println("Prototype instance");
    }
}
```

In this case, each time `PrototypeBean` is requested, a new instance is created.

Advantages of prototype scope:

- Each request gets a new instance, making it suitable for stateful components.

- Independence between bean instances.

Disadvantages:

- Higher memory usage and object creation overhead.

##### 2.1.3. Request Scope

The **Request** scope is specific to web applications. In this scope, a bean instance is created for each HTTP request and destroyed at the end of the request. This scope is useful for components that need to maintain a state throughout a single request.

Example of request scope:

```java
@Component
@Scope("request")
public class RequestBean {
```

```
    public void doSomething() {

        System.out.println("Request instance");

    }
}
```

Each time a new HTTP request is sent to the application, a new instance of `RequestBean` is created, which will only be available for that request.

##### 2.1.4. Session Scope

The **Session** scope is also specific to web applications. In this case, the bean instance is created once per user session and destroyed when the session ends. It is useful for components that need to maintain a state throughout the user session.

Example of session scope:

```java
@Component
@Scope("session")
public class SessionBean {
    public void doSomething() {
        System.out.println("Session instance");
    }
}
```

Each user that starts a new session will get a new instance of `SessionBean`, which will be maintained throughout the session.

##### 2.1.5. Application Scope

The **Application** scope is similar to the singleton scope but is used in web application contexts. In this case, a single instance of the bean is shared for the entire application lifecycle (similar to the servlet application context).

Example of application scope:

```java
@Component
@Scope("application")
public class ApplicationBean {
    public void doSomething() {
        System.out.println("Application instance");
    }
}
```

This bean is created once and shared across all requests and sessions during the application's lifetime.

##### 2.1.6. WebSocket Scope

The **WebSocket** scope is specific to handling WebSocket connections in Spring-based WebSocket applications. In this case, the bean instance is created and maintained for the entire duration of a WebSocket connection.

---

### Bean Lifecycle

The **bean lifecycle** in Spring represents the entire process a bean goes through, from creation to destruction. This lifecycle is managed by Spring's IoC container and can be customized through various techniques, such as implementing callback interfaces or using specific annotations.

#### 3.1. Bean Lifecycle Phases

The bean lifecycle in Spring can be broken down into the following main phases:

1. **Bean creation**: The IoC container creates an instance of the bean. Depending on the bean's scope (e.g., singleton or prototype), this phase may occur at application startup or when the bean is requested.

2. **Dependency injection**: Once the bean is created, the container injects all necessary dependencies specified in the bean. This can be done through constructors, setters, or fields.

3. **Initialization phase**: After the dependencies are injected, the bean enters the initialization phase. Spring provides various ways to customize this phase, including the use of the `InitializingBean` interface or the

`@PostConstruct` annotation.

4. **Bean usage**: Once the bean is initialized, it is ready to be used within the application. At this point, the bean is fully configured, and all dependencies have been injected.

5. **Destruction phase**: When the application ends, or the bean is no longer needed (e.g., in the case of a prototype scope), the bean is destroyed. This phase can also be customized through the use of the `DisposableBean` interface or the `@PreDestroy` annotation

.

#### 3.2. Customizing the Bean Lifecycle

Spring provides several ways to customize the lifecycle of a bean:

- **`@PostConstruct` and `@PreDestroy` annotations**: These annotations allow you to define methods that should be called after the bean is created and before it is destroyed.

Example:

```java
@Component
public class LifecycleBean {

    @PostConstruct
    public void init() {
        System.out.println("Bean is initializing");
    }

    @PreDestroy
    public void destroy() {
```

```
        System.out.println("Bean is being destroyed");
    }
}
```

- **`InitializingBean` and `DisposableBean` interfaces**: These interfaces allow beans to define custom initialization and destruction methods by implementing `afterPropertiesSet()` and `destroy()` methods.

Example:

```java
@Component
public class LifecycleBean implements InitializingBean, DisposableBean {

    @Override
```

```java
    public void afterPropertiesSet() throws Exception {
        System.out.println("Bean is initializing");
    }

    @Override
    public void destroy() throws Exception {
        System.out.println("Bean is being destroyed");
    }
}
```

- **`@Bean(initMethod, destroyMethod)`**: When using Java-based configuration, you can specify initialization and destruction methods directly in the `@Bean` annotation.

Example:

```java
@Configuration
public class AppConfig {

    @Bean(initMethod = "init", destroyMethod = "cleanup")
    public MyBean myBean() {
        return new MyBean();
    }
}
```

In this example, the `init()` method is called after the bean is created, and the `cleanup()` method is called before the bean is destroyed.

---

By understanding and leveraging these bean

management techniques, developers can control how Spring handles the creation, usage, and destruction of objects in their application, ensuring that components are used efficiently and appropriately throughout the application lifecycle.

## 5. Spring Configuration and AOP

The Spring Framework is known for its flexibility, allowing developers to configure applications in various ways. There are three main configuration methods that Spring supports:

1. **XML Configuration**: This is the traditional method of configuration in Spring, where beans and their dependencies are declared in an XML file.

2. **Annotation-based Configuration**: This method leverages Java annotations to declare beans and their dependencies.

3. **Java Config-based Configuration**: A more modern approach that uses Java classes to configure beans.

Each of these methods has its advantages and limitations, and the choice of configuration style often depends on developer preferences or project requirements. Let's examine each option in detail.

---

### 1. XML Configuration

#### 1.1. Introduction to XML Configuration

The traditional method for configuring beans in Spring is through the use of XML files. This method was one of the first introduced in Spring and is still widely used in many legacy applications. In an XML file, developers define beans and their dependencies using XML tags. This approach separates the application's configuration from the code itself, improving modularity and flexibility.

#### 1.2. Basic Structure of an XML Configuration

A Spring XML configuration file contains a `<beans>` section that wraps all the bean definitions and other configurations. Each bean is defined using the `<bean>` element, which specifies the bean type (class) and can include information on properties and dependencies.

Here's an example of a basic XML configuration file:

```xml
<beans xmlns="http://www.springframework.org/schema/beans"

xmlns:xsi="http://www.w3.org/2001/XMLSchema-instance"

xsi:schemaLocation="http://www.springframework.org/schema/beans

http://www.springframework.org/schema/bean
```

```
    s/spring-beans.xsd">


    <!-- Bean definition -->

    <bean id="myBean" class="com.example.MyBean">

        <!-- Bean property definition -->

        <property name="property1" value="SomeValue"/>

    </bean>


    <!-- Another bean with a dependency -->

    <bean id="anotherBean" class="com.example.AnotherBean">

        <property name="dependency" ref="myBean"/>

    </bean>


</beans>
```

In this example:

- The first bean `myBean` is an instance of the `MyBean` class with a property named `property1`.

- The second bean `anotherBean` depends on `myBean`, and this dependency is injected using `ref`.

#### 1.3. Dependency Injection with XML

Spring allows for dependency injection via constructor or setter, even when using XML. Let's look at both approaches.

##### 1.3.1. Setter-based Injection

In the previous example, setter injection is done using the `<property>` element. This method is useful when there is a setter method for the dependency.

```xml
<bean id="myBean" class="com.example.MyBean">
    <property name="property1" value="SomeValue"/>
</bean>
```

In this case, Spring will call the `setProperty1()` method to set the value of `SomeValue`.

##### 1.3.2. Constructor-based Injection

Constructor injection is used when a bean requires a dependency in its constructor. In this case, the `<constructor-arg>` element is used.

Here's an example:

```xml
<bean id="myBean" class="com.example.MyBean">
   <constructor-arg name="property1" value="SomeValue"/>
</bean>
```

In this example, Spring will call the constructor of `MyBean` and pass `SomeValue` as an argument.

#### 1.4. Advantages and Disadvantages of XML Configuration

**Advantages**:

- **Modularity**: Configuration is separate from the code, making it easier to manage and maintain.

- **Compatibility**: Many legacy projects use XML, and it is supported across all versions of Spring.

- **Centralized configuration**: All bean definitions are contained in a single file or a few files, making it easier to locate and modify configurations.

**Disadvantages**:

- **Verbose**: XML configuration can become very verbose, especially in large projects.

- **Maintenance**: In large projects, maintaining XML configuration can become complex and difficult to understand.

- **Less flexible** than Java or annotation-based configurations.

---

### 2. Annotation-based Configuration

#### 2.1. Introduction to Annotation-based Configuration

Annotation-based configuration is a more modern and compact way to configure a Spring application. The main idea is to eliminate the need for XML configuration files and instead use annotations directly in the source code to define beans and dependencies. This approach is particularly popular with Spring Boot.

With annotations, you can declare beans, inject dependencies, and manage other configurations without the need to explicitly define everything in XML.

#### 2.2. Key Annotations

Spring provides several annotations to

facilitate bean management and configuration. Some of the most common annotations include:

- **@Component**: Indicates that a class is a Spring-managed bean.

- **@Autowired**: Used to automatically inject dependencies into beans.

- **@Configuration**: Used to indicate that a class contains bean definitions.

- **@Bean**: Used within a class annotated with `@Configuration` to declare a bean.

#### 2.3. Example of Annotation-based Configuration

Here's an example of configuration using annotations:

```java
import
```

org.springframework.stereotype.Component;

```
@Component
public class MyBean {
    public void doSomething() {
        System.out.println("Bean via annotation");
    }
}
```

In this case, the class `MyBean` is annotated with `@Component`, which declares this class as a Spring bean.

To inject this bean into another class:

```java
import
```

```java
org.springframework.beans.factory.annotation.Autowired;
import org.springframework.stereotype.Component;


@Component
public class AnotherBean {

    private final MyBean myBean;

    @Autowired
    public AnotherBean(MyBean myBean) {
        this.myBean = myBean;
    }

    public void performAction() {
        myBean.doSomething();
    }
}
```

```

The `@Autowired` annotation indicates that Spring should automatically inject an instance of `MyBean` into the constructor of `AnotherBean`.

#### 2.4. Stereotype-based Configuration

In addition to `@Component`, Spring offers other specialized annotations known as **stereotypes**. These annotations provide additional semantic meaning to the class:

- **@Service**: Indicates a business logic service.

- **@Repository**: Indicates a DAO (Data Access Object) component interacting with persistence.

- **@Controller**: Indicates an MVC controller in web applications.
```

#### 2.5. Advantages and Disadvantages of Annotation-based Configuration

**Advantages**:

- **Compact**: Using annotations reduces the verbosity compared to XML configuration.

- **Maintainability**: Configurations are closer to the code itself, simplifying reading and managing.

- **Reduced risk of errors**: By keeping the definitions directly in the code, the risk of inconsistencies between configuration and code is minimized.

**Disadvantages**:

- **Less separation of concerns**: Since the configuration is embedded in the code, the separation between logic and configuration can be less clear.

- **Not suitable for complex

configurations**: In some cases, especially in large projects, annotation-based configuration can become difficult to manage.

---

### 3. Java Config-based Configuration

#### 3.1. Introduction to Java Config-based Configuration

Java-based configuration in Spring is a more recent method that uses Java classes to configure beans and dependencies. Instead of using XML or explicit annotations, the configuration is performed in Java classes with methods annotated with `@Bean`. This approach offers full control over the lifecycle and configuration of beans using the power of the Java language.

#### 3.2. Defining a Java-based

Configuration

To use Java-based configuration, you create a class annotated with `@Configuration` that contains methods annotated with `@Bean` to define beans.

Here's an example of Java-based configuration:

```java
import org.springframework.context.annotation.Bean;
import org.springframework.context.annotation.Configuration;

@Configuration
public class AppConfig {
```

```
    @Bean
    public MyBean myBean() {
        return new MyBean();
    }

    @Bean
    public AnotherBean anotherBean(MyBean myBean) {
        return new AnotherBean(myBean);
    }
}
```

In this example:

- The `AppConfig` class is annotated with `@Configuration`, indicating that this class contains bean definitions.

- The methods annotated with `@Bean` define the beans themselves. When Spring invokes `myBean()`, it will create and manage an instance of `MyBean`.

#### 3.3. Advantages and Disadvantages of Java-based Configuration

**Advantages**:

- **Flexibility**: Configurations can be fully dynamic and based on Java logic. You can use control flow constructs like `if` and `for`.

- **Testability**: Java-based configurations can be easier to test, as configuration classes can be instantiated directly.

- **Modularity**: Java-based configuration can be divided into multiple configuration classes, making it easier to manage large projects.

**Disadvantages**:

- **Less intuitive for new users**: Less experienced developers may find Java configuration more difficult to grasp compared to XML or annotations.

- **Less declarative**: Java-based configuration is more imperative compared to annotations, which may make it less readable in very large projects.

---

### AOP (Aspect-Oriented Programming)

**Aspect-Oriented Programming (AOP)** is a programming paradigm that focuses on separating cross-cutting concerns, such as logging, security, and transaction management, which can affect different parts of an application. The main idea of AOP is to separate these cross-cutting concerns from the business code, improving modularity and making the code easier to maintain.

#### 1. Introduction to AOP

In a typical application, there are cross-cutting

concerns that are not specific to a single module or component

. Examples include logging, transaction management, and security. Implementing these concerns directly within the business logic can lead to code that is hard to maintain and test.

AOP provides a way to modularize these concerns, allowing them to be applied across multiple modules without modifying the core business logic. This leads to cleaner, more modular code.

#### 2. Key Concepts in AOP

- **Aspect**: A module that encapsulates a concern that cuts across multiple components, such as logging.

- **Join Point**: A point in the program's execution where an aspect can be applied. In Spring AOP, this is typically a method invocation.

- **Advice**: The action that is taken by an aspect at a specific join point. There are different types of advice, such as "before", "after", and "around" advice.

- **Pointcut**: A set of join points where an aspect should be applied. Pointcuts allow you to specify when and where aspects should be woven into the code.

- **Weaving**: The process of applying aspects to the target code. In Spring AOP, weaving typically occurs at runtime.

#### 3. Example of AOP in Spring

In Spring, AOP is typically implemented using annotations or XML configuration. Here's an example of using AOP with annotations to log method invocations.

First, define an aspect class:

```java
import org.aspectj.lang.annotation.Aspect;
import org.aspectj.lang.annotation.Before;
import org.springframework.stereotype.Component;

@Aspect
@Component
public class LoggingAspect {

    @Before("execution(* com.example.MyBean.*(..))")
    public void logBefore() {
        System.out.println("Method is about to be called.");
    }
}
```

In this example:

- The `LoggingAspect` class is annotated with `@Aspect`, indicating that this class is an aspect.

- The `@Before` annotation specifies that the `logBefore()` method should be executed before any method in the `MyBean` class is invoked.

This aspect will be automatically applied to any method execution within the `MyBean` class, adding logging without modifying the business logic.

#### 4. Types of Advice

- **Before advice**: Executed before the method invocation.

- **After advice**: Executed after the method invocation, regardless of its outcome.

- **Around advice**: Wraps the method invocation, allowing you to control whether the method is executed or not.

- **After Returning advice**: Executed only if the method completes successfully.

- **After Throwing advice**: Executed only if the method throws an exception.

#### 5. Advantages and Disadvantages of AOP

**Advantages**:

- **Separation of concerns**: AOP allows you to modularize concerns that are scattered across different parts of the codebase.

- **Improved code readability**: By removing cross-cutting concerns from the business logic, the code becomes more focused and easier to read.

- **Reusable aspects**: Aspects can be reused across multiple modules or applications.

**Disadvantages**:

- **Learning curve**: AOP can be difficult to understand, especially for developers who are new to the concept.

- **Debugging complexity**: The added indirection can make debugging more difficult, as it's not always clear when an aspect will be applied.

- **Performance overhead**: In some cases, AOP can introduce performance overhead due to the additional processing required for weaving.

---

### Conclusion

Spring offers various configuration options, each with its strengths and weaknesses. XML-based configuration is more modular but verbose, annotation-based configuration is more compact but can blur the separation of concerns, and Java-based configuration offers flexibility but may be harder to grasp for beginners. Additionally, Spring AOP provides a powerful way to manage cross-cutting concerns, improving modularity and maintainability but requiring a deeper understanding of its concepts.

# 6. Transaction Management in Spring

Transaction management is a crucial aspect of enterprise application development, especially when interacting with databases or other resources that require consistency and integrity. Spring offers a powerful transaction management framework that simplifies both programmatic and declarative transaction management.

#### 1. Basic Transaction Concepts

A **transaction** is a unit of work that must be executed atomically. In other words, a transaction must either complete entirely or not at all. Transactions are essential to ensure that operations on data are consistent and reliable. Transactions follow these properties, known as **ACID**:

- **Atomicity**: All operations within a transaction must succeed, or the transaction is rolled back, and the data returns to its previous state.

- **Consistency**: The transaction must bring the system from one valid state to another valid state, preserving data integrity.

- **Isolation**: Concurrent transactions must be executed in a way that the outcome of one transaction is not visible to others until it is completed.

- **Durability**: Once a transaction is completed, the changes must be permanent, even in the event of a system failure.

#### 2. Configuring Transaction Management in Spring

Spring supports transaction management at both the code level (programmatic transactions) and the declarative level (declarative transactions). Basic configuration for transaction management in Spring requires using a `PlatformTransactionManager` and proper configuration of the datasource.

##### 2.1. XML Configuration

If using XML configuration, transaction management is set up in the `applicationContext.xml` file or a dedicated transaction configuration XML file.

Example of XML configuration:

```xml
<beans xmlns="http://www.springframework.org/schema/beans"

xmlns:xsi="http://www.w3.org/2001/XMLSchema-instance"

xmlns:tx="http://www.springframework.org/schema/tx"
```

```xml
xsi:schemaLocation="http://www.springframework.org/schema/beans

http://www.springframework.org/schema/beans/spring-beans.xsd

http://www.springframework.org/schema/tx

http://www.springframework.org/schema/tx/spring-tx.xsd">

    <!-- Datasource configuration -->
    <bean id="dataSource" class="org.apache.commons.dbcp2.BasicDataSource">
        <property name="driverClassName" value="com.mysql.cj.jdbc.Driver"/>
        <property name="url" value="jdbc:mysql://localhost:3306/mydb"/>
        <property name="username" value="user"/>
        <property name="password"
```

```xml
        value="password"/>
    </bean>

    <!-- Transaction manager configuration -->
    <bean id="transactionManager" class="org.springframework.jdbc.datasource.DataSourceTransactionManager">
        <property name="dataSource" ref="dataSource"/>
    </bean>

    <!-- Enabling transaction management -->
    <tx:annotation-driven transaction-manager="transactionManager"/>

</beans>
```

In this example:

- A `BasicDataSource` is configured for connecting to the database.

- A `DataSourceTransactionManager` is set up to manage transactions.

- Transaction management is enabled using annotations with `<tx:annotation-driven>`.

##### 2.2. Java Config

Java configuration is more modern and flexible. Here's an example of transaction management configuration using Java Config:

```java
import org.springframework.context.annotation.Bean;
import org.springframework.context.annotation.Configuration;
import org.springframework.jdbc.datasource.DataSou
```

rceTransactionManager;

import org.springframework.transaction.PlatformTransactionManager;

import org.springframework.transaction.annotation.EnableTransactionManagement;

import javax.sql.DataSource;

```java
@Configuration
@EnableTransactionManagement
public class AppConfig {

    @Bean
    public DataSource dataSource() {
        // Configure and return the datasource
    }

    @Bean
```

```
    public PlatformTransactionManager transactionManager(DataSource dataSource) {
        return new DataSourceTransactionManager(dataSource);
    }
}
```

In this example:

- `@EnableTransactionManagement` enables annotation-based transaction management.

- `transactionManager` creates and returns a `DataSourceTransactionManager`.

#### 3. Using the `@Transactional` Annotation

Spring supports declarative transaction management through the `@Transactional` annotation. This annotation can be applied to methods or classes to automatically manage transactions.

##### 3.1. `@Transactional` Annotation

The `@Transactional` annotation can be applied to methods or classes to indicate that operations should be executed within a transaction. Here's an example:

```java
import org.springframework.stereotype.Service;
import org.springframework.transaction.annotation.Transactional;

@Service
public class UserService {

    @Transactional
```

```
    public void registerUser(User user) {

        // Logic to register the user

        userRepository.save(user);


        // Additional logic interacting with the database

    }
}
```

In this example:

- The `@Transactional` annotation on the `registerUser` method indicates that this method should be executed within a transaction.

- If an exception occurs during the method execution, the transaction is automatically rolled back, and any changes to the database are undone.

##### 3.2. `@Transactional` Annotation Properties

The `@Transactional` annotation supports various properties that can be configured to control transaction behavior:

- **propagation**: Defines how a transaction behaves when an existing transaction is already present. Examples: `REQUIRED`, `REQUIRES_NEW`, `NESTED`.

- **isolation**: Defines the isolation level of the transaction. Examples: `READ_COMMITTED`, `SERIALIZABLE`.

- **timeout**: Specifies the timeout in seconds for the transaction.

- **readOnly**: Indicates if the transaction is read-only, optimizing performance for read operations.

Example of advanced configuration:

```java
import org.springframework.transaction.annotation.Isolation;
import org.springframework.transaction.annotation.Propagation;
import org.springframework.transaction.annotation.Transactional;


@Transactional(propagation = Propagation.REQUIRES_NEW, isolation = Isolation.SERIALIZABLE, timeout = 30, readOnly = false)
public void processTransaction() {
    // Logic for processing the transaction
}
```

---

This provides an overview of transaction management in Spring, including both XML and Java configuration options, as well as the use of the `@Transactional` annotation for declarative transaction management.

# 7.Spring Data and Security

**Spring Data** is a Spring project that simplifies data access and management in Java applications by providing a set of tools and conventions for interacting with various data sources, such as relational and NoSQL databases. Its primary goal is to reduce boilerplate code and simplify integration with different data stores, supporting technologies like JPA, MongoDB, Cassandra, and many more.

#### 1. Introduction to Spring Data

Spring Data offers several modules that streamline interaction with different persistence technologies, automating many common operations. Some of the key modules include:

- **Spring Data JPA**: For interacting with relational databases using the Java Persistence

API (JPA).

- **Spring Data MongoDB**: For working with MongoDB, a NoSQL document-based database.

- **Spring Data Redis**: For interacting with Redis, an in-memory data structure store.

- **Spring Data Elasticsearch**: For interacting with Elasticsearch, a search and analytics engine.

One of the main features of Spring Data is the use of repositories, which provide a simple, declarative way to access data, reducing the need to write manual SQL or JPQL code.

#### 2. Repositories and CRUD Operations

A **Repository** in Spring Data is an interface that extends one of the several base interfaces provided by the framework, such as `JpaRepository` or `MongoRepository`. These interfaces offer predefined methods for performing CRUD (Create, Read, Update,

Delete) operations without needing to write detailed implementations.

##### 2.1. Creating a Repository with Spring Data JPA

To use Spring Data JPA, you need to define an entity class and a repository interface.

**Entity Definition:**

```java
import javax.persistence.Entity;
import javax.persistence.GeneratedValue;
import javax.persistence.GenerationType;
import javax.persistence.Id;

@Entity
public class User {
```

```
    @Id
    @GeneratedValue(strategy = GenerationType.IDENTITY)
    private Long id;

    private String username;
    private String password;
    private String email;

    // Getters and setters
}
```

**Repository Definition:**

```java
import org.springframework.data.jpa.repository.JpaR
```

epository;

```
public interface UserRepository extends JpaRepository<User, Long> {
    // Custom methods can be defined here
    User findByUsername(String username);
}
```

In this example:

- `@Entity` indicates that `User` is a JPA entity class.

- `@Id` and `@GeneratedValue` are used to define the primary key and the generation strategy.

- `UserRepository` extends `JpaRepository`, which provides predefined CRUD methods and allows the definition of custom queries like `findByUsername`.

##### 2.2. CRUD Operation Examples

Once the repository is defined, you can use the provided methods to perform CRUD operations.

**Creating and Saving a New User:**

```java
import org.springframework.beans.factory.annotation.Autowired;
import org.springframework.stereotype.Service;

@Service
public class UserService {

    @Autowired
    private UserRepository userRepository;
```

```java
    public User createUser(String username, String password, String email) {
        User user = new User();
        user.setUsername(username);
        user.setPassword(password);
        user.setEmail(email);
        return userRepository.save(user);
    }
}
```

**Finding a User by Username:**

```java
public User findUserByUsername(String username) {
    return userRepository.findByUsername(username);
```

}
```

**Updating a User:**

```java
public User updateUser(Long id, String newEmail) {
    User user = userRepository.findById(id).orElseThrow(() -> new RuntimeException("User not found"));
    user.setEmail(newEmail);
    return userRepository.save(user);
}
```

**Deleting a User:**

```java

```
public void deleteUser(Long id) {
    userRepository.deleteById(id);
}
```

#### 3. JPA Configuration with Spring Data

To configure JPA with Spring Data, you need to set up the data source and transaction manager. Spring Boot simplifies this by automating many necessary settings, but here's an example of manual configuration.

##### 3.1. Configuring DataSource and JPA in a Spring Boot Application

**Configuration via `application.properties` or `application.yml`:**

```properties
```

# application.properties

```
spring.datasource.url=jdbc:mysql://localhost:3306/mydb
spring.datasource.username=root
spring.datasource.password=secret
spring.jpa.hibernate.ddl-auto=update
spring.jpa.show-sql=true
```

**JPA Configuration in a Configuration Class:**

```java
import org.springframework.context.annotation.Bean;
import org.springframework.context.annotation.Configuration;
import
```

```java
org.springframework.data.jpa.repository.config.EnableJpaRepositories;

import org.springframework.orm.jpa.JpaTransactionManager;

import org.springframework.orm.jpa.LocalContainerEntityManagerFactoryBean;

import org.springframework.orm.jpa.vendor.HibernateJpaVendorAdapter;

import org.springframework.transaction.PlatformTransactionManager;


import javax.persistence.EntityManagerFactory;

import javax.sql.DataSource;


@Configuration

@EnableJpaRepositories(basePackages = "com.example.repository")
```

```java
public class JpaConfig {

    @Bean
    public LocalContainerEntityManagerFactoryBean entityManagerFactory(DataSource dataSource) {

        LocalContainerEntityManagerFactoryBean emf = new LocalContainerEntityManagerFactoryBean();
        emf.setDataSource(dataSource);
        emf.setJpaVendorAdapter(new HibernateJpaVendorAdapter());

        emf.setPackagesToScan("com.example.model");
        return emf;
    }

    @Bean
```

```
    public PlatformTransactionManager transactionManager(EntityManagerFactory entityManagerFactory) {

        return new JpaTransactionManager(entityManagerFactory);

    }
}
```

In this example:

- `LocalContainerEntityManagerFactoryBean` configures the `EntityManagerFactory`.

- `PlatformTransactionManager` handles JPA transactions.

---

### Security with Spring Security

**Spring Security** is a powerful and highly customizable framework for securing Java applications, providing features like authentication, authorization, protection against common attacks such as CSRF and XSS, session management, and role-based access control.

#### 1. Introduction to Spring Security

Spring Security integrates seamlessly with the Spring Framework and offers out-of-the-box security features. Some of the main concepts include:

- **Authentication**: The process of verifying a user's identity.

- **Authorization**: Determining access permissions for an authenticated user.

- **Security Filters**: Components that intercept HTTP requests to apply security measures.

#### 2. Configuring Security Rules

Spring Security can be configured in various ways, but the most common approach is through Java Config.

##### 2.1. Basic Configuration with Spring Security

**Security Configuration Class:**

```java
import org.springframework.context.annotation.Bean;
import org.springframework.context.annotation.Configuration;
import org.springframework.security.config.annotation.web.builders.HttpSecurity;
import
```

org.springframework.security.config.annotation.web.builders.AuthenticationManagerBuilder;

import org.springframework.security.config.annotation.web.configuration.EnableWebSecurity;

import org.springframework.security.core.userdetails.UserDetailsService;

import org.springframework.security.core.userdetails.User;

import org.springframework.security.core.userdetails.UsernameNotFoundException;

import org.springframework.security.provisioning.InMemoryUserDetailsManager;

import org.springframework.security.web.SecurityFilterChain;

@Configuration

```java
@EnableWebSecurity
public class SecurityConfig extends WebSecurityConfigurerAdapter {

    @Override
    protected void configure(HttpSecurity http) throws Exception {
        http
            .authorizeRequests()
                .antMatchers("/public/**").permitAll()
                .anyRequest().authenticated()
                .and()
            .formLogin()
                .loginPage("/login")
                .permitAll()
                .and()
            .logout()
                .permitAll();
```

```java
    }

    @Override
    protected void configure(AuthenticationManagerBuilder auth) throws Exception {
        auth
            .inMemoryAuthentication()
                .withUser("user").password("{noop}password").roles("USER")
                .and()
                .withUser("admin").password("{noop}admin").roles("ADMIN");
    }
}
```

In this example:

- `configure(HttpSecurity http)` defines access rules for HTTP requests. Requests to `/public/**` are permitted for everyone, while all other requests require authentication.

- `configure(AuthenticationManagerBuilder auth)` configures in-memory authentication with two users: `user` and `admin`.

##### 2.2. Authentication and Authorization

**Authentication:**

Spring Security provides multiple ways to authenticate users, including in-memory, database-based, and external service authentication.

**Authorization:**

Once authenticated, Spring Security applies authorization rules based on the user's roles or other properties.

**Database-Based Authentication Example:**

```java
import org.springframework.context.annotation.Bean;
import org.springframework.context.annotation.Configuration;
import org.springframework.security.config.annotation.web.builders.HttpSecurity;
import org.springframework.security.config.annotation.web.builders.AuthenticationManagerBuilder;
import org.springframework.security.core.userdetails.UserDetailsService;
import org.springframework.security.provisioning.JdbcUserDetailsManager;
```

```java
import javax.sql.DataSource;

@Configuration
public class SecurityConfig extends WebSecurityConfigurerAdapter {

    @Bean
    public UserDetailsService userDetailsService(DataSource dataSource) {
        return new JdbcUserDetailsManager(dataSource);
    }

    @Override
    protected void configure(AuthenticationManagerBuilder auth) throws Exception {
        auth
            .jdbcAuthentication()
                .dataSource(dataSource())
```

```
            .usersByUsernameQuery("SELECT username, password, enabled FROM users WHERE username = ?")

            .authoritiesByUsernameQuery("SELECT username, role FROM user_roles WHERE username = ?");
    }
}
```

In this example:

- `JdbcUserDetailsManager` is used to manage database-based user authentication.

- `dataSource()` configures the connection to the database.

#### 3. Role-Based Authorization

**Role-Based Authorization Example:**

```java
import org.springframework.security.access.prepost.PreAuthorize;
import org.springframework.stereotype.Service;

@Service
public class AdminService {

    @PreAuthorize("hasRole('ROLE_ADMIN')")
    public void performAdminTask() {
        // Only users with the ADMIN role can access this method
    }
}
```

In this example:

`@PreAuthorize("hasRole('ROLE_ADMIN')")` ensures that only users with the ADMIN role can access the performAdminTask method.

Spring Data and Spring Security provide powerful tools for data management and application security. Spring Data simplifies data interaction by reducing boilerplate code and enhancing developer productivity, while Spring Security offers a comprehensive, customizable framework for securing applications against unauthorized access and managing authentication and authorization. Together, these tools help build robust, secure, and scalable applications with Spring.

Here's the English translation of the provided text:

# 8. Testing Spring Applications

Testing is a crucial part of software development that ensures the code works as expected and that changes do not introduce regressions. Spring provides robust support for testing applications through integration with JUnit, Mockito, and other testing libraries. This support helps test various components of the application, including Spring components, repositories, services, and controllers.

#### 1. Introduction to Testing in Spring

The Spring testing framework is designed to simplify writing and running unit and integration tests. Spring provides various annotations and support classes that facilitate testing framework components, configuring the test environment, and isolating tests.

**Key Testing Annotations:**

- **`@SpringBootTest`**: Loads the entire Spring application context for integration tests.

- **`@DataJpaTest`**: Configures a test environment for JPA repositories, providing a test configuration for data access.

- **`@WebMvcTest`**: Configures a test environment for Spring MVC controllers, loading only the necessary parts for controller tests.

- **`@MockBean`**: Allows creating and injecting mocks into Spring context beans.

**Example of Test Configuration:**

```java
import org.junit.jupiter.api.Test;

import org.springframework.beans.factory.annotation.Autowired;

import org.springframework.boot.test.autoconfigure.
```

web.servlet.WebMvcTest;

import org.springframework.test.web.servlet.MockMvc;

import org.springframework.test.web.servlet.request.MockMvcRequestBuilders;

import org.springframework.test.web.servlet.result.MockMvcResultMatchers;

@WebMvcTest(MyController.class)

public class MyControllerTest {

   @Autowired

   private MockMvc mockMvc;

   @Test

   public void testGreeting() throws Exception {

```
mockMvc.perform(MockMvcRequestBuilders.get("/greeting"))

.andExpect(MockMvcResultMatchers.status().isOk())

.andExpect(MockMvcResultMatchers.content().string("Hello, World!"));
    }
}
```

In this example:

- `@WebMvcTest` creates a test environment for the specified controller.

- `MockMvc` is used to simulate HTTP requests and verify responses.

#### 2. Using JUnit and Mockito

JUnit is the most common framework for unit testing in Java, while Mockito is a library for creating mock objects, which can be used to isolate code units during tests.

##### 2.1. JUnit

JUnit is used to write and run unit tests. The latest version is JUnit 5, which includes new concepts and improvements over JUnit 4.

**Example of a Unit Test with JUnit:**

```java
import org.junit.jupiter.api.Test;
import static org.junit.jupiter.api.Assertions.assertEquals;

public class MathServiceTest {
```

```java
    @Test
    public void testAddition() {
        MathService mathService = new MathService();
        int result = mathService.add(2, 3);
        assertEquals(5, result, "2 + 3 should equal 5");
    }
}
```

In this example:

- `@Test` indicates that the method is a test.

- `assertEquals` verifies that the expected result and the actual result are equal.

##### 2.2. Mockito

Mockito is a library that facilitates the

creation of mock objects and defining expected behaviors for those objects. It is particularly useful for testing isolated components, such as services and repositories, without depending on their dependencies.

**Example of Using Mockito:**

```java
import org.junit.jupiter.api.Test;
import org.mockito.InjectMocks;
import org.mockito.Mock;
import org.mockito.MockitoAnnotations;
import static org.mockito.Mockito.*;
import static org.junit.jupiter.api.Assertions.*;

public class UserServiceTest {

    @Mock
```

```java
    private UserRepository userRepository;

    @InjectMocks
    private UserService userService;

    @Test
    public void testFindUserByUsername() {
        MockitoAnnotations.openMocks(this);
        User user = new User("john_doe", "password");

        when(userRepository.findByUsername("john_doe")).thenReturn(user);

        User result = userService.findUserByUsername("john_doe");
        assertEquals("john_doe", result.getUsername());
    }
```

```
}
```

In this example:

- `@Mock` creates a mock of `UserRepository`.

- `@InjectMocks` creates an instance of `UserService` and injects the mock `UserRepository` into it.

- `when` defines the behavior of the mock.

- `assertEquals` verifies that the result of the method call is as expected.

#### 3. Testing Spring Components

Testing Spring components ensures that application components, such as services, controllers, and repositories, function correctly within the Spring application context.

##### 3.1. Testing Services

Services can be tested using `@SpringBootTest` to load the entire application context or using a more specific test context.

**Example of Testing a Service:**

```java
import org.junit.jupiter.api.Test;
import org.springframework.beans.factory.annotation.Autowired;
import org.springframework.boot.test.context.SpringBootTest;

@SpringBootTest
public class UserServiceIntegrationTest {
```

```java
    @Autowired
    private UserService userService;

    @Autowired
    private UserRepository userRepository;

    @Test
    public void testCreateUser() {
        User user = userService.createUser("john_doe", "password", "john@example.com");
        assertNotNull(user.getId());
        assertEquals("john_doe", user.getUsername());
    }
}
```

In this example:

- `@SpringBootTest` loads the entire application context.

- The test verifies that the created user has a non-null ID and the correct username.

##### 3.2. Testing Controllers

Controllers can be tested using `MockMvc` to simulate HTTP requests and verify responses.

**Example of Testing a Controller:**

```java
import org.junit.jupiter.api.Test;

import org.springframework.beans.factory.annotation.Autowired;

import org.springframework.boot.test.autoconfigure.
```

```java
web.servlet.WebMvcTest;
import org.springframework.test.web.servlet.MockMvc;
import org.springframework.test.web.servlet.request.MockMvcRequestBuilders;
import org.springframework.test.web.servlet.result.MockMvcResultMatchers;

@WebMvcTest(UserController.class)
public class UserControllerTest {

    @Autowired
    private MockMvc mockMvc;

    @Test
    public void testGetUser() throws Exception {
```

```
mockMvc.perform(MockMvcRequestBuilders.get("/users/1"))

.andExpect(MockMvcResultMatchers.status().isOk())

.andExpect(MockMvcResultMatchers.jsonPath("$.username").value("john_doe"));
    }
}
```

In this example:

- `@WebMvcTest` configures the test environment for the controller.

- `MockMvc` is used to simulate a GET request and verify that the result is correct.

---

### Microservices with Spring Boot

**Spring Boot** is a Spring project that simplifies the creation and configuration of Spring applications, making it easier to start new applications with minimal configuration. It is particularly useful for creating microservices, which are small, autonomous, and independent services.

#### 1. What is Spring Boot?

Spring Boot provides a convention-over-configuration architecture and default settings that reduce the complexity of manual configuration. It also offers a range of tools and libraries for building production-ready applications.

**Key Features of Spring Boot:**

- **Auto-Configuration**: Spring Boot automatically configures the application based on dependencies present in the classpath.

- **Starter Projects**: Starter projects are dependencies that provide default configuration for specific purposes.

- **Actuator**: Provides monitoring and management endpoints for production applications.

- **Embedded Servers**: Supports embedded servers like Tomcat, Jetty, and Undertow, eliminating the need for separate server configuration.

#### 2. Creating a Spring Boot Application

Creating a Spring Boot application is straightforward thanks to Spring Initializr, an online tool that generates the base project with the required dependencies.

##### 2.1. Using Spring Initializr

1. **Visit [Spring Initializr](https://start.spring.io/)**.

2. **Select Options**: Specify the project type (Maven or Gradle), Spring Boot version, project name, and necessary dependencies (e.g., Web, JPA, H2).

3. **Generate the Project**: Click "Generate" to download a ZIP file with the base project.

##### 2.2. Example Spring Boot Application

**Main Class:**

```java
import org.springframework.boot.SpringApplication;
import org.springframework.boot.autoconfigure.SpringBootApplication;

@SpringBootApplication
public class MyApplication {
```

```java
public static void main(String[] args) {
    SpringApplication.run(MyApplication.class, args);
    }
}
```

**Controller:**

```java
import org.springframework.web.bind.annotation.GetMapping;
import org.springframework.web.bind.annotation.RequestMapping;
import org.springframework.web.bind.annotation.RestController;
```

```
@RestController
@RequestMapping("/api")
public class MyController {

    @GetMapping("/hello")
    public String sayHello() {
        return "Hello, World!";
    }
}
```

In this example:

- `@SpringBootApplication` is the main annotation that enables auto-configuration and component scanning.

- `MyController` handles a GET request and returns a "Hello, World!" response.

#### 3. Configuration and Dependency Management

Spring Boot simplifies dependency management through starter projects and auto-configuration.

##### 3.1. Dependencies via Maven

Dependencies can be managed in the `pom.xml` file.

**Example of `pom.xml`:**

```xml
<dependencies>
  <dependency>
<groupId>org.springframework.boot</groupId>
```

```xml
    <artifactId>spring-boot-starter-web</artifactId>
  </dependency>
  <dependency>
    <groupId>org.springframework.boot</groupId>
    <artifactId>spring-boot-starter-data-jpa</artifactId>
  </dependency>
  <dependency>
    <groupId>org.h2</groupId>
    <artifactId>h2</artifactId>
    <scope>runtime</scope>
  </dependency>
  <dependency>
    <groupId>org.springframework.boot</groupId>
```

            d>

    <artifactId>spring-boot-starter-test</artifactId>

    <scope>test</scope>

  </dependency>

</dependencies>
```

##### 3.2. Configuration via `application.properties`

Configuration settings are managed in the `application.properties` or `application.yml` file.

**Example of `application.properties`:**

```properties
server.port=8080

```
spring.datasource.url=jdbc:h2:mem:testdb
spring.datasource.username=sa
spring.datasource.password=password
spring.jpa.hibernate.ddl-auto=update
```

In this example:

- `server.port` configures the server port.

- `spring.datasource.url` specifies the database connection URL.

- `spring.jpa.hibernate.ddl-auto` configures the Hibernate schema generation strategy.

#### 4. Building Microservices with Spring Boot

Spring Boot's features make it well-suited for developing microservices, which are small, independently deployable services that communicate over a network.

##### 4.1. Microservice Example

A typical microservice includes a REST controller, service layer, and repository layer.

**Controller:**

```java
@RestController
@RequestMapping("/api/users")
public class UserController {

    @Autowired
    private UserService userService;

    @GetMapping("/{id}")
    public User getUser(@PathVariable Long id) {
```

```
        return userService.findById(id);
    }
}
```

**Service:**

```java
@Service
public class UserService {

    @Autowired
    private UserRepository userRepository;

    public User findById(Long id) {
        return userRepository.findById(id).orElse(null);
    }
```

}
```

**Repository:**

```java
import org.springframework.data.jpa.repository.JpaRepository;

public interface UserRepository extends JpaRepository<User, Long> {
}
```

In this example:

- The `UserController` exposes REST endpoints for user operations.

- The `UserService` contains business logic.
```

- The `UserRepository` handles data access.

##### 4.2. Communicating Between Microservices

Microservices often need to communicate with each other using REST APIs or messaging queues. Spring Boot provides tools and libraries for both methods.

**Example of REST Communication:**

```java
import org.springframework.stereotype.Service;
import org.springframework.web.client.RestTemplate;

@Service
```

```java
public class ExternalServiceClient {

    private final RestTemplate restTemplate;

    public ExternalServiceClient(RestTemplate restTemplate) {
        this.restTemplate = restTemplate;
    }

    public User getUserById(Long id) {
        return restTemplate.getForObject("http://external-service/api/users/" + id, User.class);
    }
}
```

In this example:

- `RestTemplate` is used to make HTTP

requests to another microservice.

#### 5. Monitoring and Management

Spring Boot Actuator provides built-in endpoints to monitor and manage the application.

##### 5.1. Enabling Actuator

To enable Actuator, add the dependency to `pom.xml`:

```xml
<dependency>
    <groupId>org.springframework.boot</groupId>
    <artifactId>spring-boot-starter-actuator</artifactId>
```

        </dependency>
```

##### 5.2. Accessing Actuator Endpoints

Actuator provides various endpoints, such as `/actuator/health` and `/actuator/metrics`, to monitor application health and metrics.

**Example of accessing Actuator endpoints:**

```bash
curl http://localhost:8080/actuator/health
```

**Response:**

```json

```
{
    "status": "UP"
}
```

In this example:

- The `/actuator/health` endpoint provides the application's health status.

# 9.Spring Glossary

Spring is a powerful framework for Java that simplifies enterprise application development. Below is a glossary of key terms and components used in Spring, along with practical examples.

---

#### **1. Bean**

A **bean** is an object managed by the Spring container. Beans are instantiated, configured, and managed by Spring based on definitions provided in XML, annotations, or Java Config.

**Example:**

```java
```

```java
import org.springframework.stereotype.Component;

@Component
public class MyService {
  public void serve() {
     System.out.println("Service is serving...");
  }
}
```

Here, `@Component` marks `MyService` as a Spring-managed bean.

---

#### **2. Dependency Injection (DI)**

**Dependency Injection** is a design pattern where the Spring container injects an object's dependencies rather than the object creating them itself, enhancing modularity and testability.

**Example:**

```java
import org.springframework.beans.factory.annotation.Autowired;
import org.springframework.stereotype.Service;

@Service
public class MyController {

    private final MyService myService;
```

```
    @Autowired
    public MyController(MyService myService) {
        this.myService = myService;
    }

    public void handleRequest() {
        myService.serve();
    }
}
```

In this example, `@Autowired` injects `MyService` into `MyController`.

---

#### **3. Inversion of Control (IoC)**

**Inversion of Control** is a principle where control over application flow is inverted from the application's code to the Spring container. This is closely related to Dependency Injection.

**Example:**

```xml
<beans xmlns="http://www.springframework.org/schema/beans"

xmlns:xsi="http://www.w3.org/2001/XMLSchema-instance"

xsi:schemaLocation="http://www.springframework.org/schema/beans

http://www.springframework.org/schema/beans/spring-beans.xsd">
```

```
    <bean id="myService" class="com.example.MyService"/>

    <bean id="myController" class="com.example.MyController">
        <constructor-arg ref="myService"/>
    </bean>
</beans>
```

In this XML configuration, `MyController` is injected with `MyService`.

---

#### **4. Application Context**

The **Application Context** is the central container in Spring that manages bean creation, configuration, and lifecycle. It also provides dependency management.

**Example:**

```java
import org.springframework.context.annotation.AnnotationConfigApplicationContext;

public class App {
    public static void main(String[] args) {
        AnnotationConfigApplicationContext context = new AnnotationConfigApplicationContext(AppConfig.class);
        MyController controller = context.getBean(MyController.class);
        controller.handleRequest();
        context.close();
    }
}
```

```

Here, `AnnotationConfigApplicationContext` is used to create a context from the configuration class `AppConfig`.

---

#### **5. Aspect-Oriented Programming (AOP)**

**Aspect-Oriented Programming** allows separation of cross-cutting concerns (like logging or transaction management) from the main application logic. In Spring, AOP is used to manage these aspects.

**Example:**

```java

```java
import org.aspectj.lang.annotation.Aspect;
import org.aspectj.lang.annotation.Before;
import org.springframework.stereotype.Component;

@Aspect
@Component
public class LoggingAspect {

    @Before("execution(* com.example.MyService.*(..))")
    public void logBeforeMethod() {
        System.out.println("Method is about to be called...");
    }
}
```

`LoggingAspect` executes before every

method in `MyService`.

---

#### **6. Spring Boot**

**Spring Boot** is an extension of Spring that simplifies the setup and configuration of Spring applications. It provides defaults and auto-configuration options to quickly create production-ready applications.

**Example:**

```java
import org.springframework.boot.SpringApplication;
import org.springframework.boot.autoconfigure.SpringBootApplication;
```

```
@SpringBootApplication
public class Application {
    public static void main(String[] args) {
        SpringApplication.run(Application.class, args);
    }
}
```

`@SpringBootApplication` enables auto-configuration and component scanning.

---

#### **7. Spring Data**

**Spring Data** provides abstractions for data access and interaction with various databases. It supports repositories for JPA, MongoDB, Redis, and more.

**Example:**

```java
import org.springframework.data.jpa.repository.JpaRepository;

public interface UserRepository extends JpaRepository<User, Long> {
    User findByUsername(String username);
}
```

`UserRepository` extends `JpaRepository` to support CRUD operations and custom queries.

---

#### **8. Transaction Management**

**Transaction Management** in Spring ensures data consistency by managing transactions in a declarative or programmatic manner.

**Example:**

```java
import org.springframework.stereotype.Service;
import org.springframework.transaction.annotation.Transactional;

@Service
public class UserService {
```

```
    @Transactional
    public void createUser(User user) {
        // Operations to create a user
    }
}
```

`@Transactional` ensures that operations within `createUser` method are performed within a transaction.

---

#### **9. Spring MVC**

**Spring MVC** is a framework for building web applications following the Model-View-Controller pattern, managing HTTP requests, and rendering responses.

**Example:**

```java
import org.springframework.stereotype.Controller;
import org.springframework.web.bind.annotation.GetMapping;
import org.springframework.web.bind.annotation.RequestMapping;

@Controller
@RequestMapping("/api")
public class MyController {

   @GetMapping("/hello")
   public String hello() {
      return "hello";
   }
```

}
```

`MyController` handles GET requests to `/api/hello` and returns the view name `hello`.

---

#### **10. Spring Security**

**Spring Security** is a framework that provides authentication, authorization, and protection against common security vulnerabilities.

**Example:**

```java
import org.springframework.context.annotation.Confi

guration;

import org.springframework.security.config.annotation.web.builders.HttpSecurity;

import org.springframework.security.config.annotation.web.configuration.EnableWebSecurity;

import org.springframework.security.config.annotation.web.configuration.WebSecurityConfigurerAdapter;

@Configuration

@EnableWebSecurity

public class SecurityConfig extends WebSecurityConfigurerAdapter {

  @Override

  protected void configure(HttpSecurity http) throws Exception {

    http

```
        .authorizeRequests()
        .antMatchers("/admin/**").hasRole("ADMIN")
        .antMatchers("/user/**").hasRole("USER")
            .and()
        .formLogin();
    }
}
```

`SecurityConfig` configures security rules, allowing access to `/admin/**` for `ADMIN` role and `/user/**` for `USER` role.

---

#### **11. Aspect**

An **aspect** is a module that defines a cross-cutting concern which can be applied to various points in an application. Aspects in Spring AOP manage concerns such as logging and transaction management.

**Example:**

```java
import org.aspectj.lang.annotation.Aspect;
import org.aspectj.lang.annotation.Before;
import org.springframework.stereotype.Component;

@Aspect
@Component
public class MyAspect {

    @Before("execution(* com.example.MyService.*(..))")
```

```
    public void beforeMethod() {
        System.out.println("Method is about to be executed...");
    }
}
```

`MyAspect` is an aspect that executes `beforeMethod` before every method in `MyService`.

---

#### **12. Join Point**

A **join point** is a specific point during the execution of an application where an aspect can be applied. Examples include method calls or object instantiations.

**Example:**

```java
import org.aspectj.lang.JoinPoint;
import org.aspectj.lang.annotation.After;
import org.aspectj.lang.annotation.Aspect;
import org.springframework.stereotype.Component;

@Aspect
@Component
public class LoggingAspect {

    @After("execution(* com.example.MyService.*(..))")
    public void afterMethod(JoinPoint joinPoint) {
        System.out.println("Executed method: " + joinPoint.getSignature().getName());
```

       }
}
```

Here, `JoinPoint` provides details about the method executed after its completion.

---

#### **13. Pointcut**

A **pointcut** is an expression that defines the join points where advice should be applied. Pointcuts select specific join points in the application flow.

**Example:**

```java

```java
import org.aspectj.lang.annotation.Aspect;
import org.aspectj.lang.annotation.Pointcut;
import org.springframework.stereotype.Component;

@Aspect
@Component
public class MyAspect {

    @Pointcut("execution(* com.example.MyService.*(..))")
    public void serviceMethods() {}

    @Before("serviceMethods()")
    public void beforeServiceMethods() {
        System.out.println("Before executing service method...");
    }
}
```

`serviceMethods` is a pointcut that matches all methods in `MyService`.

---

#### **14. Advice**

**Advice** is the action taken by an aspect at a join point. It can be executed before, after, or around the join point.

**Example:**

```java
import org.aspectj.lang.annotation.Aspect;
import org.aspectj.lang.annotation.After;
import org.aspectj.lang.annotation.Before;
```

```java
import org.aspectj.lang.annotation.Around;
import org.aspectj.lang.ProceedingJoinPoint;
import org.springframework.stereotype.Component;

@Aspect
@Component
public class MyAspect {

    @Before("execution(* com.example.MyService.*(..))")
    public void beforeAdvice() {
        System.out.println("Before advice...");
    }

    @After("execution(* com.example.MyService.*(..))")
    public void afterAdvice() {
        System.out.println("After advice...");
```

```java
    }

    @Around("execution(* com.example.MyService.*(..))")
    public Object aroundAdvice(ProceedingJoinPoint joinPoint) throws Throwable {
        System.out.println("Around advice - before...");
        Object result = joinPoint.proceed();
        System.out.println("Around advice - after...");
        return result;
    }
}
```

In this example, `beforeAdvice` runs before, `after

Advice` runs after, and `aroundAdvice` runs before and after the join point.

---

#### **15. Auto-configuration**

**Auto-configuration** in Spring Boot automatically configures your application based on the dependencies present in the classpath. It simplifies setup with sensible defaults.

**Example:**

```java
import org.springframework.boot.SpringApplication;
import org.springframework.boot.autoconfigure.SpringBootApplication;
```

```
@SpringBootApplication
public class Application {
    public static void main(String[] args) {
        SpringApplication.run(Application.class, args);
    }
}
```

`@SpringBootApplication` enables auto-configuration and component scanning.

---

#### **16. Profiles**

**Profiles** in Spring allow you to define different configurations for various environments (e.g., development, testing, production). You can activate profiles to load specific configurations.

**Example:**

```java
import org.springframework.context.annotation.Bean;
import org.springframework.context.annotation.Configuration;
import org.springframework.context.annotation.Profile;

@Configuration
public class AppConfig {

    @Bean
```

```
    @Profile("dev")
    public MyService devService() {
        return new MyServiceDev();
    }

    @Bean
    @Profile("prod")
    public MyService prodService() {
        return new MyServiceProd();
    }
}
```

Different beans are created depending on whether the `dev` or `prod` profile is active.

---

#### **17. Actuator**

**Actuator** is a Spring Boot module that provides endpoints for monitoring and managing applications in production. It includes features like health checks and metrics.

**Example:**

```yaml
# application.yml
management:
  endpoints:
    web:
      exposure:
        include: '*'
```

In this configuration, all Actuator endpoints are exposed for management and monitoring.

# Index

1. Introduction to Spring pg.4

2. Setting Up the Development Environment pg.17

3. Fundamental Concepts of Spring pg.34

4. Bean Management in Spring pg.51

5. Spring Configuration and AOP pg.75

6. Transaction Management in Spring pg.101

7. Spring Data and Security pg.114

# 8.Testing Spring Applications pg.139

# 9.Spring Glossary pg.170

www.ingramcontent.com/pod-product-compliance
Lightning Source LLC
Chambersburg PA
CBHW071051240526
45471CB00015B/1639